SCHOLASTIC

Read, Snack & Learn
With
Favorite Picture Books

by Jodi Simpson

The Grouchy Ladybug
by Eric Carle

Freight Train
by Donald Crews

NEW YORK • TORONTO • LONDON • AUCKLAND • SYDNEY
MEXICO CITY • NEW DELHI • HONG KONG • BUENOS AIRES

Teaching
Resources

DEDICATION

To my children, Casey and Sky, thank you for sharing your favorite stories with me, over and over again. Together we have traveled the world, lived adventures, laughed, cried, and fallen in love with characters and settings, without ever leaving the comfort of the green chair or your cozy beds. To my husband, Craig, thank you for supporting me and cheering me on as I sat night after night working to get the words just right.

Cover design by Maria Lilja
Cover photography by James Levin
Cover and interior artwork by Maxie Chambliss

Interior design by Holly Grundon

ISBN: 0-439-51186-0
Copyright © 2004 by Jodi Simpson

2 3 4 5 6 7 8 9 10   40   11 10 09 08 07 06 05 04

Contents

Book Titles and Authors	Snack Recipes	

Introduction

Welcome to *Read, Snack & Learn With Favorite Picture Books!* I've been sharing stories with children for over 10 years as a mother, library storyteller, preschool teacher, and currently as a first-grade teacher. Sharing literature is my passion, and finding ways to help young readers connect with a story is an exciting challenge. Through my students, I've discovered that we never want the stories we read to be over. After all, who can say goodbye to the cat in Dr. Seuss's *The Cat in the Hat* or the caterpillar from Eric Carle's *The Very Hungry Caterpillar?* We embrace picture books, holding onto memorable characters and the stories that frame them long after we say "the end."

In this book, I've included many ways to keep the learning going, ways to celebrate 18 stories through literacy-building activities and fun, no-cook recipes. You'll find ideas for introducing and exploring the books and for using easy-to-read rebus recipes to make ladybug apples, graham cracker trains, tortilla pinwheel flowers, and more. The reproducible recipes are something special that children can read and prepare as a group, in small groups, or independently.

So, join me in bringing storybooks to life with scrumptious snacks. It's as I always say, *What could be as tasty as a good book? How about a yummy snack!*

—JODI SIMPSON

How to Use This Book

*For each featured picture book and recipe
there is an activity-based Teacher Page, broken
down into three sections—Before Reading,
After Reading, and Making the Snack.*

> **Before Reading**

*To set the stage for reading aloud with students,
choose ideas from the Picnic Basket Preview or
the Knowledge Web sections. Each offer teaching
suggestions specific to the book you're reading.*

Picnic Basket Preview

It's fun to have a picnic basket for this activity, but any large basket will do just fine. Inside the basket place the book you'll be reading aloud with children, plus items related to the story. For example, you might introduce Bill Martin, Jr.'s *Brown Bear, Brown Bear, What Do You See?* by tucking a teddy bear and a variety of fruit inside your picnic basket. Build students' anticipation for reading by showing them one object from the basket at a time. After the class has had a few minutes to make observations about the objects, invite children to make predictions about what the story might be about. Then, read the book aloud with children.

Knowledge Web

Before reading the story aloud, use a graphic organizer shaped like a web to record what children already know about a book or subject, accessing their background knowledge, broadening their associations with the story, and laying the groundwork for comprehension. Begin by making observations about the book's cover, title, and author. Then, in a circle that will be the central focus of the web, write the title of the book or the concept you'll be exploring. Draw lines that extend outward from the circle. At the end of each, write the smaller ideas. With each Knowledge Web book activity, you'll find a webbing example to get you started.

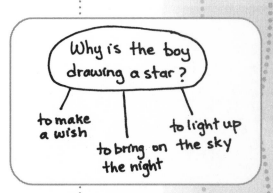

After Reading

*Use either or both of these activities
to take a closer look at the story.*

Discussion Starters

Evaluate and deepen reading comprehension with questions and comments that serve as springboards for discussion. Consider using chart paper to record students' observations, opinions, comparisons, and so on.

Language Link

Build literacy skills with this activity that invites students to examine the story's text, providing opportunities for exploring unfamiliar words, synonyms, descriptive language, and more.

Making the Snack

*This section contains helpful tips
for making the snack.*

Ahead of Time

Turn to these time-saving suggestions before you even gather the ingredients. This is where you'll learn what needs to be prepared in advance and why. Plus, you'll find advice regarding distributing ingredients to students.

Teaching With the Recipe

When you're ready to create the snack, make a photocopy of the recipe for each student and distribute it to children. Explain that the words and pictures on the recipe page indicate the steps they will follow to assemble the snack. As a group, read the recipe aloud, pointing out the rebus clues and how-to illustrations as you go along. Spend a few minutes showing students the ingredients, tools, and materials they'll be using. For an extra dash of support, ask volunteers to retell what happens at each step of the process before the class begins making their snacks.

Make Connections

Use the language found in this section to identify links between the book children read and the snack they will prepare.

Highlight Strategies for Success

These tips invite students to problem solve and share what they know about using measuring tools and handling food safely.

Revisit Learning
In this section, you'll find quick suggestions for sharing and reviewing what children have learned.

Ingredients
Take a peek at this box on the Teacher Page to find out exactly what you need and how much of it you need per child.

Tools & Materials
Make cooking in the classroom easier by having all the tools and materials you'll need close at hand. The items listed in the Tools & Materials box are key to snack-time success—from the measuring spoons you'll need for setup to the paper plates on which students will assemble the majority of their snacks.

A Few Health & Safety Guidelines

Check health records and/or send a note home to ask families about children's food allergies. In some cases you may have to adjust a recipe to meet a child's needs and sensitivities. Make substitutions as needed.

Wash and dry all fruit and vegetables in advance of preparing the snack.

Keep all perishables in the refrigerator as long as possible before preparation.

Clean work surfaces before and after food preparation, with a cleaning solution recommended by your school or district.

Have students wash their hands with soap and water and then dry them with paper towels before and after any food handling.

Store leftovers in airtight containers, in a refrigerator as necessary.

Food for Thought

Snack time in the classroom can be an informative and eye-opening experience, as the children in your class may possess a wide array of cultural and religious backgrounds. Consider students' food preferences, traditions, and beliefs as you present the snack recipes. Help children find the commonalities between what they eat and how they eat. What may seem like an ordinary snack to one student may seem surprising to another.

Activities for Teaching With Any Book

The following activities build reading skills and support language learning. They are in addition to the activities that accompany each of the titles and recipes featured in this book.

Introduce the Book With a Story Apron

Here's a different spin on the Picnic Basket Preview (see page 5). Instead of using a picnic basket to present a book, use an apron with surprises in its pockets. Any apron with pockets can be a story apron. Tie on the apron and tuck objects related to the story inside the pockets. Then, whet students' appetites for reading the story by showing them one object at a time. If you're introducing *Animal Tracks*, you might place a few small stuffed animals in the apron pockets. After the class has had a few minutes to think about the different objects, invite children to make predictions about what the story might be about.

Write a Letter to a Storybook Character

Let a shared reading experience be a springboard for shared writing. After reading the book aloud, invite students to compose a letter to a character or group of characters from the story. Record children's letter writing on chart paper. For instance, after reading about the two girls in *The Apple Pie Tree*, you might write something like the letter below.

> *Dear Kids,*
> *Our class just read The Apple Pie Tree. How lucky you are to have an apple pie tree in your yard! We don't have an apple tree in our classroom but we do have some applesauce and granola bars. We are going to use those ingredients to make pies just like yours.*
>
> *From,*
> *Mrs. Simpson's First Graders*

Alphabetize Recipe Ingredients

Write a recipe's ingredients on large index cards, one item per card. For example, for the *Snowman Faces* recipe you'll need six index cards. The words you'll need are: *rice cakes, cream cheese, raisins, cheese, carrots,* and *almonds*. Mix up the cards and have students help you place the cards in alphabetical order, securing the words with clothespins onto a length of string. Let children know that these are the ingredients the class will be using to prepare the snack. Hang the list vertically. When it's time to go through the rebus directions on the recipe page, invite volunteers to point out familiar words.

Order Recipe Sentence Strips in a Pocket Chart

Turn reading the recipe aloud into a learning-filled pocket chart activity. Begin by showing students the recipe the class will use to make a snack. When children have become familiar with it, ask them to retell you each of the recipe's steps. Record each step on a sentence strip, modeling sounding out and leaving spaces between words. Place the strips in order in a pocket chart. Encourage children to refer to the pocket chart during snack making, reinforcing language learning and new vocabulary.

Chef Hats

Turn the classroom into the bustling kitchen of a fine restaurant! Invite students to wear chefs' hats as they prepare their snacks. To make the chefs' hats, begin by photocopying one copy of the pattern on page 64 for each child. To increase the hats' durability, laminate the pages before distributing the pattern to students. Then, have the young chefs follow the directions below.

1. Cut out the hat pattern along the outer solid cut lines.

2. Cut out the bands that go around the head.

3. Tape the bands onto the back of the chef's hat.

4. Adjust the band to fit around the head and tape the bands together. (Children may need assistance with this step. Consider having each child work with a partner to fit and tape the hat in place.)

Engage Readers With Chef Puppets

Turn any puppet or soft animal toy into a chef puppet you can use as a helpful teaching prop. Begin by making a copy of the template on page 64, and by using a photocopier's reduction or enlargement feature to make a chef's hat that fits well. Then, cut out the pattern and follow the directions above for making the chef's hat.

Use your chef puppet to introduce a picture book, share the contents of the picnic basket, read a story aloud, or introduce a snack recipe. You might use the puppet to think aloud with students, guiding children through reading the recipe's rebus directions and problem solving through each step.

Swimmy

by Leo Lionni (Pantheon, 1963)

A clever little fish creates a way for himself and his friends to escape the hungry jaws of a big fish.

Before Reading

Picnic Basket Preview

Place a copy of the book and a bag of fish-shaped crackers inside your picnic basket. Show both items to students. Ask children to think about what the fish-shaped crackers might have to do with the book. Ask, *Why would fish-shaped crackers be a good snack to go with this story?* Then, encourage children to imagine and discuss the kinds of adventures a small fish might find in the ocean.

Knowledge Web

Help students share what they know about fish, how they look, and what the different parts of a fish are named. Familiarizing children with what fish actually look like will come in handy later when it's time to make a snack. As a group, discuss the book's cover,

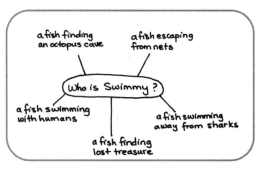

title, and author. Then, invite students to offer predictions about who Swimmy might be. Record their ideas on chart paper. (See example, above.)

After Reading

Discussion Starters

Encourage students to identify the different steps the fish had to go through to form themselves into one big fish. Talk about the way all the fish had to work together for protection. Discuss the importance of cooperation and how it makes good things happen for everyone involved.

Language Link

List ways that students cooperate with each other in school to make good things happen. How do children share, take turns, and help one another? Ask, *Why is it better to cooperate than not to cooperate? What problems do we avoid when we do cooperate?*

Making the Snack

Ahead of Time

You may wish to give children a large fish-shaped pattern to use as a template for drawing a fish on their plates. Place the fish-shaped crackers into large bowls that the children can scoop from when they are measuring out their crackers.

Teaching With the Recipe

Make Connections

Consider saying something like the following: *What a clever fish! I was surprised to see how Swimmy cooperated with his friends to disguise themselves into one big fish. Let's make our very own big fish of little fish crackers!*

Highlight Strategies for Success

Invite volunteers to share what they know about drawing fish, that a fish has a head, tail, and fins. To make sure students draw a large fish on their plates you might say, *Draw a fish a little bit bigger than your hand.* If students draw their fish too small, their crackers won't fit inside the shape.

Revisit Learning

Encourage students to share what they learned about how small fish protect themselves from predators. (It took a lot of small fish working together to scare away larger fish.)

Ingredients

(FOR EACH CHILD)

1 cup fish-shaped crackers

1 fish-shaped pretzel

Tools & Materials

(FOR EACH CHILD)

recipe on page 12

1 orange crayon

1 one-cup measuring cup (per group)

1 paper plate

Schools of Fish

1 **Use** a crayon 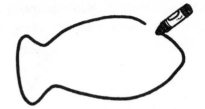 to draw the outline of a big fish 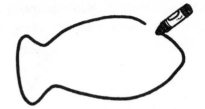 .

2 **Measure** 1 cup of crackers  .

3 **Arrange** the crackers  to cover the fish  .

4 **Place** one pretzel fish  to make an eye.

The Apple Pie Tree

by Zoe Hall (Scholastic, 1996)

A brother and sister watch their apple pie tree change through the seasons. When autumn comes the apples ripen and the children are finally able to make apple pies.

Before Reading

Picnic Basket Preview

In your picnic basket, place the book, applesauce, granola bars, and a pie tin. Before reading the story, discuss the book's cover. Look at the artwork and invite children to predict what the book might be about. Then, show the items in the basket. Encourage children to predict what the snack will be. *Which words from the title are clues about our snack?*

Knowledge Web

Show students the book you'll be reading. Talk about the story's cover and title. On chart paper, write "Apple Pie Tree" in the circle that will be the central focus of the web. Ask children to predict what they think an apple pie tree really is, based on what they already know about trees, apples, and baking. (See example, right.)

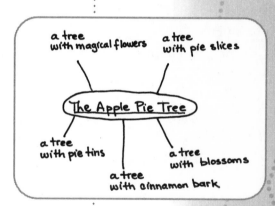

After Reading

Discussion Starters

Have students sequence the story in order of the seasons, beginning with winter. As a group, talk about what types of changes children noticed in the tree and the baby robins. Then use chart paper to record two columns of information, "changes in the tree," and "changes in the robins." Ask students to describe and compare the ways the seasons impacted the tree and the robins.

Language Link

Turn to the book's last page for information about how apples grow. Read aloud each step of an apple's growth. Then, draw children's attention to some of the page's nonfiction text structures, such as the heading, numbered diagrams, and boldfaced words. Record the boldfaced words (*pollen, nectar, pollination,* and *apple*) on chart paper. As a group, develop definitions for each.

Ingredients
(FOR EACH CHILD)

1 vanilla wafer cookie

4 tablespoons applesauce

1/2 crunchy-style cinnamon granola bar

Tools & Materials
(FOR EACH CHILD)

recipe on page 15

1 medium-sized bowl (per group)

1 baking cup

1 measuring spoon (per group)

1 plastic self-sealing plastic bag

1 paper plate

Ahead of Time

Pour the applesauce into the bowls for groups of children to use for measuring applesauce. Some children have difficulty in digesting apples, so you may want to provide yogurt or pudding to use as a substitution.

Teaching With the Recipe

Make Connections

Consider saying something like the following: *The characters in the story made a traditional apple pie, but we get to make a new type of apple pie. Let's see how our recipe is a little bit the same and a little bit different from the recipe in the book.*

Highlight Strategies for Success

Invite volunteers to share what they know about cooking with drippy ingredients like applesauce and crumbly ingredients like granola. *How should we hold our tablespoons as we measure applesauce? How can we keep the granola from spilling out of the bag while we're breaking the bar into little pieces?*

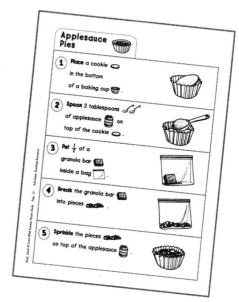

Revisit Learning

Encourage students to share what they learned about seasons, apple trees, and making (and eating!) applesauce pies.

Applesauce Pies

1 **Place** a cookie in the bottom of a baking cup.

2 **Spoon** 2 tablespoons of applesauce on top of the cookie.

3 **Put** $\frac{1}{2}$ of a granola bar inside a bag.

4 **Break** the granola bar into pieces.

5 **Sprinkle** the pieces on top of the applesauce.

Brown Bear, Brown Bear, What Do You See?

by Bill Martin, Jr. (Henry Holt & Company, 1983)

Brightly colored animals of all sorts look right back at the reader of this engaging story.

Before Reading

Picnic Basket Preview

Pack your basket with a copy of the book, a teddy bear, and fruit: strawberries, oranges, golden delicious apples, and green grapes. The teddy bear is always a hit with children and becomes "Brown Bear" from the story. Use the bear to introduce the story and to examine its cover with students (and have the bear do the talking). Explain that the book is all about animals and colors. As a quick review of color words, try a chant like this: *First graders, first graders, what do you see?* Have children reply, *I see red strawberries looking at me.* Repeat the questioning and answering process with the orange oranges, yellow apples, and green grapes.

Knowledge Web

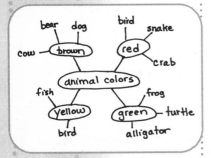

As a group, discuss the book's cover, title, and author. Invite students to share what they know about animals and what colors we find them in. For example, most children have seen a green turtle, yellow duck, and brown horse. Record colors and corresponding animal names in a web. Refer to the words as needed for building color word recognition. (See example, left.)

After Reading

Discussion Starters

Go back through the story at least two more times. See if children can remember, without looking, which animals were which colors. Make a list of guesses on chart paper. Then, go through the book together and record the actual colors and animals. Talk about the results.

Language Link

Invite children to name fruits and vegetables we describe with color words (green beans, orange carrots, and yellow lemons). Challenge students to come up with more examples. Then, let children know they will use some brightly colored fruits to make a tasty snack.

Ahead of Time

Slice the apples, divide the oranges into segments, and remove stems from the strawberries. Each group will need a bowl of each as well as a bowl of green grapes. Then, draw a bear face on chart paper for children to use as a model for the bear face. Or, provide round-shaped templates that students can trace with brown crayon.

Teaching With the Recipe

Make Connections

Consider saying something like the following: *Did you see all those color words in our story? Let's use some of these color words to make a delicious snack. As we make our snacks we'll ask our plates, 'Bear plate, bear plate, what do you see?' Then, we'll make our bear faces with red strawberries, orange slices, yellow apples, and green grapes.*

Highlight Strategies for Success

Invite children to talk about the features on a bear's face. *Let's name the features on Brown Bear's face (eyes, ears, nose, mouth, or snout). After we draw the bear's face, we'll use the fresh fruit in this recipe to finish it.*

Revisit Learning

Encourage students to talk about their snack creations, identifying the color of each fruit. Then, talk about the other animals in the story. Invite children to name colorful fruits they could use to design edible versions of those animals.

Fresh Fruit Bears

1 **Draw** a circle ○

for the bear's face  .

2 **Place** 1 strawberry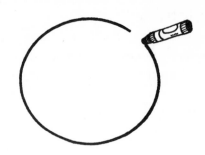

in the center for a nose.

3 **Place** 2 grapes

for his eyes.

4 **Place** 2 orange slices

for his snout.

5 **Place** 2 apple slices

for his ears.

The Teddy Bears' Picnic

by Jimmy Kennedy (Simon & Schuster, 2000)

Readers can revisit this favorite children's song by enjoying the beautiful pictures of teddy bears heading to the woods for a picnic.

Before Reading

Picnic Basket Preview

Tuck a copy of the book, a blanket, a few teddy bears, and some toy food into a basket. To introduce the story, bring the filled basket over to the reading area. Spread out the blanket for you and students to sit on for listening to the story. Hold up the book and show children the cover and ask them what they know about picnics. Tell them that to listen to this story they will be going on a pretend picnic. Invite volunteers to hold the bears and toy food as the group pretends to go into the woods for a teddy bear picnic.

Knowledge Web

Hold up the book for students to see the title and cover. Ask children to share with the group what they already know about going on picnics, what people do at picnics, and what kinds of food are often present. Record these on a web. (See example, right.)

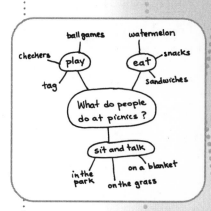

After Reading

Discussion Starters

Ask students about how the child in the story disguised himself to watch the bears at their picnic. Ask them how they would disguise themselves if they were following their teddy bears into the woods for a picnic. Record their ideas on chart paper.

Language Link

Ask children to tell you what the teddy bears at their homes would like to eat on a picnic. As a group, create a menu especially for a teddy bear picnic. On a piece of chart paper, write the headings Appetizers, Salads, Main Dishes, Side Dishes, and Desserts. Under each heading write the name of the foods children suggest. When the menu is complete, put it in a center and invite students to write appetizing descriptions beside each food item.

Ingredients

(FOR EACH CHILD)

1 celery stalk

2 tablespoons
peanut butter

20 raisins

Tools &
Materials

(FOR EACH CHILD)

recipe on page 21

1 small bowl
(per group)

1 plastic butter knife

1 paper plate

Making the Snack

Ahead of Time

Instead of counting out raisins, purchase a large box of raisins for each group of children. Prepare the celery by cutting away the leaves and ends. Set out peanut butter in the bowls, enough for each group of children to share.

Teaching With the Recipe

Make Connections

Consider saying something like the following: *Many times when a picnic is over, teeny tiny ants arrive to eat the crumbs and picnic leftovers. Let's pretend we've had a picnic and some ants have come to join us. Our ants will really be raisins.*

Highlight Strategies for Success

Invite volunteers to share some safe ways to cut celery stalks, including where to place their hands as they use the knife. As children go over the last steps of the recipe you might ask, *What are some ways we could make sure the "ants" (raisins) don't fall off the peanut butter?*

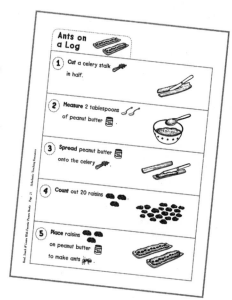

Revisit Learning

Encourage students to share what they learned about picnics, ants, and teddy bears. Many children may be familiar with the song this book is based on. For extra fun, locate the music and play the song as you show the class pages from the book.

Ants on a Log

1 **Cut** a celery stalk 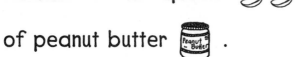 in half.

2 **Measure** 2 tablespoons  of peanut butter.

3 **Spread** peanut butter onto the celery.

4 **Count** out 20 raisins.

5 **Place** raisins on peanut butter to make ants.

Animal Tracks

by Arthur Dorros (Scholastic, 1991)

Readers become animal detectives and discover which animals have been visiting a stream bank in this informational book that asks, Who's been here?

Before Reading

Picnic Basket Preview

In the basket place a copy of the book along with a small backpack, a pair of binoculars, and a bag of trail mix. (You'll need to make some trail mix in advance.) Hold up the book and show children the contents of the picnic basket. Help children name each object in the picnic basket. When you get to the trail mix, explain that it's a healthy, easy-to-carry snack for hikers. Hiking and exploring nature can be hard work. It's helpful to have a healthy snack that gives you energy. Let students know that they will make a snack they can eat while they look for animal tracks on the playground or in a nearby park.

Knowledge Web

Introduce the book, showing children the cover, and several track-filled pages of the story. Invite children to make predictions about the book, based on what they know about

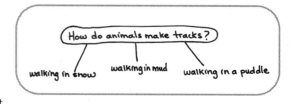

animals and wildlife footprints. Create a web that includes different ways animals leave tracks in the dirt, snow, or mud. (See example, above.)

After Reading

Discussion Starters

Invite children to share what they know about eating healthy snacks. Explain that our bodies need energy to move and think. If we fuel up our bodies with nutritious foods, we'll be able to do more hiking without getting tired. Have volunteers name some examples of healthy snacks.

Language Link

Use the animal tracks in the front and back pages of the book as inspiration for a fun matching game. To make the game, copy the tracks of six animals onto index cards. On another set of index cards, write each animal's name. Laminate all the cards for durability. Place the cards and a copy of the book in a center. Invite students to work in pairs or independently to match the words cards with the animal tracks.

Making the Snack

Ahead of Time

Put the ingredients into medium-sized bowls. Each group of children will need four bowls—peanuts, chocolate chips, raisins, and pretzels.

Teaching With the Recipe

Make Connections

Consider saying something like the following: *I wonder if the family in this story brought any trail mix with them to keep their energy up while they were hiking. We need to keep up our energy because we will be going on a hike too.*

Highlight Strategies for Success

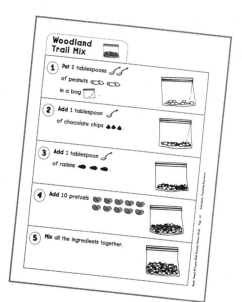

Invite volunteers to share what they know about measuring dry ingredients such as peanuts, chocolate chips, and raisins. *How should we hold our measuring spoons so the ingredients don't tumble out? No matter how carefully we work, some ingredients are sure to end up on the table. What should we do then?*

Revisit Learning

Encourage children to share what they've learned about animals and their tracks. Invite volunteers to describe their favorite animal tracks.

Ingredients

(FOR EACH CHILD)

2 tablespoons shelled peanuts

1 tablespoon chocolate chips

1 tablespoon raisins

10 mini-twist pretzels

Tools & Materials

(FOR EACH CHILD)

recipe on page 24

4 medium-sized bowls (per group)

1 plastic self-sealing sandwich bag

1 set measuring spoons (per group)

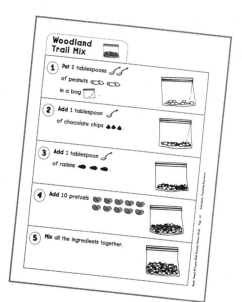

Woodland Trail Mix

1. Put 2 tablespoons of peanuts in a bag

2. Add 1 tablespoon of chocolate chips.

3. Add 1 tablespoon of raisins

4. Add 10 pretzels

5. Mix all the ingredients together.

Woodland Trail Mix

1 **Put** 2 tablespoons of peanuts in a bag .

2 **Add** 1 tablespoon of chocolate chips ▲▲▲.

3 **Add** 1 tablespoon of raisins .

4 **Add** 10 pretzels .

5 **Mix** all the ingredients together.

A House Is a House for Me

by Mary Ann Hoberman (Penguin Putnam, 1978)

Poetry and rhyme lead readers into visualizing houses in ways they've never thought of before.

MARY ANN HOBERMAN
Illustrated by BETTY FRASER

Before Reading

Picnic Basket Preview

Inside your basket, place a copy of the book, a box of graham crackers, and pictures of houses. Introduce the book by showing children the cover of the book and reading the title aloud. As a group, discuss different types of houses. Then, hold up the house pictures and talk about what materials were used to build each one. Next, show the box of graham crackers and let children know that they will be using crackers to build houses.

Knowledge Web

As a group, discuss the book's cover, title, and author. Invite students to create a web about homes, based on what they know about different kinds of buildings and the materials used to build them. Or, if you prefer, create a web of animal homes, shelters, or habitats. Encourage children to predict what types of houses might be in this book. (See example, right.)

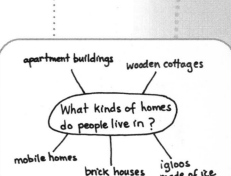

After Reading

Discussion Starters

Talk about all the imaginative ways the author described objects as being houses for various things. Provide the students with some more examples. You might say, *A radio is a house for a song. A heart is a house for love. A cow is a house for milk.* Ask children to come up with their own ideas for houses for things.

Language Link

Invite children to talk about the many steps involved in building a home. Explain that builders begin with a plan that looks like a map. They use the pictures and the words on the map to build the structure step by step. Connect this idea to the concept of following a recipe. Show a copy of the Snack Cracker House recipe to students and examine the instructions together. Then, invite children to draw a picture of what their snack house will look like. Encourage them to add words to describe each part.

Ahead of Time

Tint the frosting with any color food coloring. Use a sharp knife to cut the graham crackers into the shapes needed for the recipe—houses, roofs, chimneys, and doors. Put a set of the crackers on a paper plate with two tablespoons of frosting for each child.

Ingredients
(FOR EACH CHILD)

1 graham cracker

2 tablespoons frosting

Tools & Materials
(FOR EACH CHILD)

recipe on page 27

food coloring (per group)

1 plastic butter knife

1 paper plate

Teaching With the Recipe

Make Connections

Consider saying something like the following: *Isn't it interesting how the author thought up all those many ideas for houses for things? For our snack today, we will be making a house with a roof, a chimney, and a door.*

Highlight Strategies for Success

Invite volunteers to use the recipe page to explain the process of building a cracker house, especially how to use icing to attach the door. Ask, *How will we use our recipe's words and drawings to guide us?* Have the volunteers point out illustrations and bolded words.

Revisit Learning

Encourage students to share what they learned about different kinds of houses and homes.

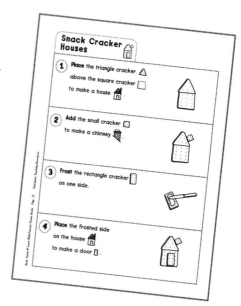

Snack Cracker Houses

1 **Place** the triangle cracker △ above the square cracker ▢ to make a house 🏠.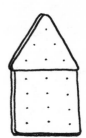

2 **Add** the small cracker ▢ to make a chimney 🏭.

3 **Frost** the rectangle cracker ▭ on one side.

4 **Place** the frosted side on the house 🏠 to make a door ▯.

Draw Me a Star

by Eric Carle (Philomel Books, 1992)

A young artist draws a star and much more, until eventually his drawings bring this delightful story full circle.

Before Reading

Picnic Basket Preview

Inside the basket, place a copy of the story, a star-shaped cookie cutter, bread, and cheese. Introduce the story by explaining that the boy begins his adventure by drawing one star. The star takes him on a journey through his life of creating more and more drawings. Show children the star-shaped cookie cutter, bread, and cheese. Explain that instead of drawing stars after reading the story, the class will be making star sandwiches.

Knowledge Web

Introduce the book by showing students its cover and the title. Have children predict what will happen in the story, based on what they know about the process of drawing stars. Ask, *Why do you think this boy is drawing a star? What will happen next?* Record their ideas on a web. (See example, left.)

After Reading

Discussion Starters

Read the students through the story again. Have them think about why the star would want a sun, or why a tree would want some people, or why people would want a house. List their ideas on chart paper.

Language Link

Reinforce students' reading skills with a pocket chart that teaches directional words. Use the drawings on page 22 of the story as inspiration. Begin by drawing the first four steps needed for creating a simple star, but make step five the last step for drawing a five-pointed star (up). Then, write these words on sentence strips: *down, over, left, right,* and *up.* Put the word strips in descending order in a pocket chart. Place the how-to drawings along the bottom of the chart. To begin, read aloud the first direction word to students (down). Have students say the word and then identify the illustration that goes with it (a vertical line). Continue matching the directional words with the how-to illustrations, until all steps are in order. Then, invite children to practice drawing stars in the air!

Making the Snack

Ahead of Time

Several days before you plan to make the snack, ask families to send in star-shaped cookie cutters for the class to borrow or even to keep. Having enough cutters on hand is a big help when making this snack, making it all the more fun for children who sometimes find it difficult to wait their turn.

Teaching With the Recipe

✐ Make Connections

Consider saying something like the following: *Instead of drawing stars, we will be cutting stars with cookie cutters. After we cut some bread stars, I'm thinking these bread stars will want some cheese stars. The cheese stars will want to be put together with the bread stars to make star sandwiches, and I'm sure we'll want to eat them all.*

✐ Highlight Strategies for Success

Show children the Star Sandwiches recipe and pages 21 and 22 of the story. You might say, *Remember when the moon asked the artist to draw a star? This numbered recipe is just like that, giving us instructions on just how to make our very own star sandwiches.* Then, draw students' attention to the numbered how-to directions in the book and on the recipe page.

✐ Revisit Learning

Encourage children to share what they learned about drawing stars and preparing star sandwiches. Then, invite them to name other objects they've learned to draw and ask, *Did someone teach you how to draw [the object]? How did they teach you? If you learned on your own, how did you figure out what you needed to do to draw it?*

Ingredients
(FOR EACH CHILD)

2 slices bread

2 slices sandwich cheese

Tools & Materials
(FOR EACH CHILD)

recipe on page 30

2 star-shaped cookie cutters (per group)

1 paper plate

Star Sandwiches

1 **Use** the cookie cutter to cut 1 star out of each slice of bread .

2 **Use** the cookie cutter to cut 1 star out of each slice of cheese .

3 **Stack** the cheese stars on top of one bread star, as shown.

4 **Place** the other bread star on top to make a sandwich.
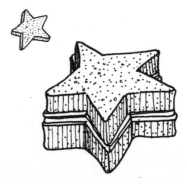

Snowballs

by Lois Ehlert (Harcourt Brace & Co., 1995)

*One snowy day, children create a snow family
like no other with stones, leaves, corn, forks,
a cap, a belt, ribbons, and even a compass.*

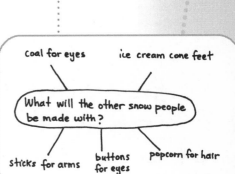

Before Reading

Picnic Basket Preview

Inside your basket place a copy of the story, mittens, and snack
ingredients (rice cakes, cream cheese, raisins, carrots, and almonds). Put on
the mittens and show children the book's cover. Invite students to predict what
the story could be about. Next, pull out the items in the basket and ask
children to think about how some people might use them to make a
snowman's face.

Knowledge Web

Ask children to guess what you might be doing if you were
outside in the snow holding a carrot. Children may guess that
you were planning to make a snowman or feeding woodland
animals. Then, show children the cover of the book and talk about
the snowman pictured. Ask, *What items did the author use to make
this snowman?* Have children predict what the other snowmen in
the book might be created with. Record their ideas on a web. (See
example, right.)

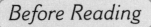

coal for eyes   ice cream cone feet

What will the other snow people
be made with?

sticks for arms   buttons   popcorn for hair
                     for eyes

After Reading

Discussion Starters

As a group, look at the page at the end of the book titled "good stuff," and
name all the items Lois Ehlert used to create her snow people. Ask
students to identify some of things they use to make their own snow people.

Language Link

The author mentions waiting for a "really big snow." Have children share
their memories of times when they've seen a really big snow. As a group,
make a list of synonyms for the word *big*. To take learning a step further, invite
children to think of words to describe a really small snow, creating a list of
antonyms for the word *big*.

Ahead of Time

Purchase small containers of soft cream cheese or set out blocks of cream cheese to soften for an hour or so before you plan to create the snack. Give each group one bowl of cream cheese to share.

Ingredients
(FOR EACH CHILD)

2 tablespoons cream cheese

1 rice cake

1 baby carrot

2 raisins

5 whole almonds

Tools & Materials
(FOR EACH CHILD)

recipe on page 33

1 small-sized bowl (per group)

1 plastic butter knife

1 paper plate

Teaching With the Recipe

Make Connections

Consider saying something like the following: *The author used such interesting objects to create her snow people and snow animals. Let's use food we can eat to transform these rice cakes into snowman faces.*

Highlight Strategies for Success

Invite volunteers to share what they know about spreading things with knives. Ask, *How should we hold the knife to spread the cream cheese safely?*

Revisit Learning

Encourage students to retell the story of the snow family. Ask, *Would the birds in the story enjoy eating these snowman snacks? Why or why not?*

Snowman Faces

1. Spread cream cheese onto a rice cake.
2. Place 1 carrot in the middle for a nose.
3. Place 2 raisins for eyes.
4. Place 5 almonds for a smile.

Snowman Faces

1 **Spread** cream cheese onto a rice cake .

2 **Place** 1 carrot 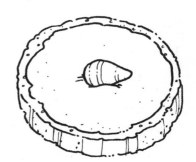 in the middle for a nose.

3 **Place** 2 raisins for eyes.

4 **Place** 5 almonds for a smile.

Freight Train

by Donald Crews (Greenwillow, 1978)

A freight train rolls along its track and into the imaginations of readers, who follow its progress through tunnels, trestles, and beyond.

Before Reading

Picnic Basket Preview

Place a copy of the book and a box of graham crackers, cream-filled chocolate cookies, and a toy train car inside your picnic basket. Show the items to students. Explain that after reading the stories, the class will be making trains using the graham crackers and the cookies. Point out the parts of the toy train, the wheels, and the body. Ask children to think about how someone could use the crackers and cookies to build a train car.

Knowledge Web

Help students share what they know about trains. Familiarizing children with what trains actually look like will come in handy later when it's time to make a snack. Then, as a group, discuss the book's cover, title, and author. Invite students to share what the different cars of a train are named, what sounds the whistles make, and how train cars sound moving along tracks. Record their ideas on chart paper. (See example, left.)

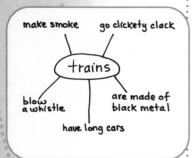

After Reading

Discussion Starters

Encourage students to share what they know about riding on passenger trains. Invite volunteers who have ridden on them to describe what a trip entails, from buying the tickets and boarding the train, to arriving at a destination and disembarking. Encourage children to think about the kinds of geographical features a train might pass on a journey (cities, tunnels, mountains). List their ideas on chart paper.

Language Link

Help build students' vocabulary by exploring words that have multiple meanings. Revisit the pages of the book, in which readers find common words such as *tender, gondola,* and *hopper* being used in ways that may be unfamiliar. Invite volunteers to copy and then illustrate each word on a separate sheet of chart paper, showing at least two definitions. For example, beneath the word *tender,* a child may draw a picture of a woman hugging a child and then another picture of a steam engine's *tender,* the car behind a steam engine that carries coal and water.

Making the Snack

Ahead of Time

Use a sharp knife to cut the graham crackers into the shapes needed for the recipe—whole crackers, half crackers, small triangle-shaped, and small square crackers. Then, cut the licorice into pieces. For each train engine you'll need 1 three-inch piece to make the curling smoke. Tint the frosting with any color food coloring. Put 2 cookies, a length of licorice, and a set of the crackers on a paper plate with 2 tablespoons of frosting for each child.

Teaching With the Recipe

 **Make Connections**

Consider saying something like the following: *The freight train in the story was made up of a rainbow of colors. For our snack today, we will be using graham crackers, cookies, frosting, and licorice to make our own colorful trains we can eat.*

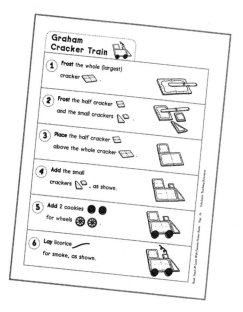

 **Highlight Strategies for Success**

Invite volunteers to use the recipe page to explain the process of assembling the train engine. Ask, *How will we use what we know about trains to guide us?* Have volunteers demonstrate how to use their fingers to curl the licorice for smoke.

 **Revisit Learning**

Encourage students to share what they learned about freight trains and different kinds of train cars.

Ingredients
(FOR EACH CHILD)

2 graham crackers

2 tablespoons frosting

3 inches black shoestring licorice

Tools & Materials
(FOR EACH CHILD)

recipe on page 36

food coloring (per group)

1 plastic butter knife

1 paper plate

Graham Cracker Train

1 **Frost** the whole (largest) cracker 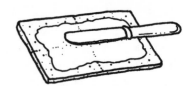 .

2 **Frost** the half cracker 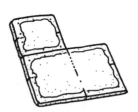 and the small crackers 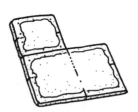 .

3 **Place** the half cracker above the whole cracker  .

4 **Add** the small crackers 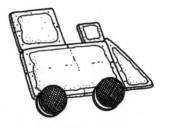 , as shown.

5 **Add** 2 cookies for wheels 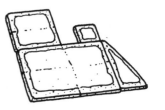 .

6 **Lay** licorice for smoke, as shown.

The Cat in the Hat Comes Back

by Dr. Seuss (Random House, 1957)

The Cat in the Hat wears out his welcome and causes all kinds of trouble—from staining Mom's new dress to staining the snow all over the yard. What a mess!

Before Reading

Picnic Basket Preview

Inside the basket, place a copy of the book, a spoon, and a Cat-in-the-Hat-type hat (or costume cat ears). Introduce the story wearing the hat. Use the spoon to pretend you are stirring something and say something like, *In this story, The Cat in the Hat stirs up some new kind of trouble. We will be stirring up some new kind of snack of our own after the story. I wonder what our snack might be!*

Knowledge Web

As a group, discuss the book's cover, title, and author. Page through the book briefly, showing children a few pictures from the story. Point out that the cat created a terrible mess. Have students think of ways a house can become cluttered, based on what they know about cleaning their own homes. Record their ideas on a web. (See example, right.)

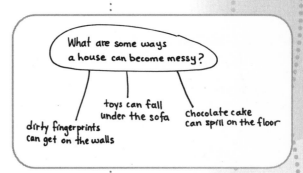

After Reading

Discussion Starters

As a group, discuss all the ways the cat made the problem of the pink ring get worse and worse. Ask children to explain what happened in sequence. *What happened first, next, and last? How did the snow get so pink?* Or, if you like, talk about the magical VOOM that cleaned up all the snow. Ask students to tell you how they would use a VOOM at their houses.

Language Link

Dr. Seuss uses fun words in his stories, creating wonderful images for readers. Explore some of the words from the story with children. Begin by writing these words on chart paper: *fast, off, hard, alone, good, stay, little,* and *deep.* Encourage students to come up with antonyms for each.

Ingredients
(FOR EACH CHILD)

1 cup plain yogurt

3 tablespoons powdered strawberry gelatin

Tools & Materials
(FOR EACH CHILD)

recipe on page 39

1 measuring cup (per group)

1 plastic bowl

1 plastic spoon

1 set of measuring spoons (per group)

Ahead of Time

Purchase large-sized tubs of yogurt and large-sized packages of gelatin, so that you can simply place one tub of yogurt and one box of gelatin out for each group of children to share.

Teaching With the Recipe

Make Connections

Consider saying something like the following: *Do you remember all the pink snow from the story? I wonder how the Cat in the Hat really did turn the snow pink. I know a way that we can turn our own pretend-snow pink. We can even eat it for a snack.*

Highlight Strategies for Success

Invite volunteers to share what they know about stirring lumpy ingredients thoroughly. *Which ingredient will make our white yogurt turn pink? How will we know when the gelatin and yogurt are all mixed together?*

Revisit Learning

Encourage students to share what they learned about making pink snow. You might ask, *How is our snow similar to or different from the snow in the book? Would the Cat in the Hat like our pink snow? Why or why not? Could the VOOM clean it up?*

Pink Yogurt Snow

1 **Measure** 1 cup of yogurt .

2 **Spoon** the yogurt into a bowl .

3 **Add** 2 tablespoons of gelatin .

4 **Mix** to make pink snow .

Ellen Stoll Walsh

Mouse Paint

by Ellen Stoll Walsh (Harcourt, 1989)

Three white mice discover the magic of mixing colors. What's more, they find ways to hide from a hungry cat.

Before Reading

Picnic Basket Preview

In your basket, place a copy of the book, three crayons (red, yellow, and blue), a bag of bagels, a package of cream cheese, and a box of food coloring. Introduce the book, by pointing out the cover and examining it with students. Then, show the crayons, food coloring, bagels, and cream cheese. Encourage students to talk about the ways colors can be mixed to create new colors. Let children know that when they make their snack, they will be mixing colors just as the mice did.

Knowledge Web

As a group, discuss the book's cover, title, and author. Ask students to think about what they know about mice, how they behave, and how we know they are around even when we can't see them. Then, invite students to guess why the mice would be mixing colors. Record their ideas on a web. (See example, right.)

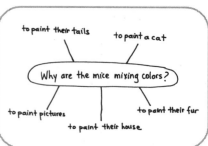

to paint their tails

to paint a cat

Why are the mice mixing colors?

to paint pictures

to paint their house

to paint their fur

After Reading

Discussion Starters

Ask children how the mice learned how to mix colors. *In the beginning of the story, what did the mice discover about mixing the colors? How were they able to trick the hungry cat?* Encourage students to use evidence from the book to support their answers.

Language Link

Build descriptive language skills with a color-naming activity. Begin by showing children a few crayons and then reading a few of the color names like apricot, sapphire, and goldenrod. Encourage children to think about how people name colors, often choosing names that remind people of something familiar. Show a few more crayons and invite children to create new names for those colors. (Paint color samples from hardware stores also work well for this activity.)

Making the Snack

Ahead of Time

Purchase small containers of soft cream cheese or set out blocks of cream cheese to soften for an hour or so before you plan to create the snack. Place two tablespoons of cream cheese into plastic bowls or drinking cups, two for each child. Provide each table of students with red, yellow, and blue food coloring to share.

Teaching With the Recipe

 **Make Connections**

Consider saying something like the following: *Those mice had fun mixing paints and creating new colors. Red and yellow make orange. Yellow and blue make green. I wonder what would happen if we mixed different colors of cream cheese instead of mixing different colors of paint together.*

 **Highlight Strategies for Success**

Invite volunteers to share what they know about working with food coloring. *Our recipe calls for one drop of each color. How can we make sure we use just one drop from each bottle?*

 **Revisit Learning**

Encourage students to share what they learned about making the colors orange and green. You might ask, *How was our mixing colors different from what the mice did in the story?*

Ingredients
(FOR EACH CHILD)

4 tablespoons cream cheese

1 whole bagel, sliced

Tools & Materials
(FOR EACH CHILD)

recipe on page 42

2 plastic bowls or drinking cups

food coloring (red, yellow, and blue) (per group)

1 plastic butter knife

Colorful Bagels

1 **Add** 1 drop of red and 1 drop of yellow food coloring to the cream cheese in one bowl.

2 **Use** a knife

to mix the cream cheese .

3 **Add** 1 drop of blue and 1 drop of yellow food coloring to the cream cheese in the other bowl.

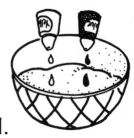

4 **Use** a knife

to mix the cream cheese .

5 **Spread** the cream cheese

onto the bagels .

The Cloud Book

by Tomie dePaola (Holiday House, 1975)

Colorful drawings and engaging text invite students to learn about the science and myths that relate to clouds.

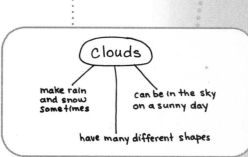

Before Reading

Picnic Basket Preview

Inside your basket, place a copy of the book along with a large sheet or blanket. Introduce the book by explaining that it is an informational story about clouds. Spread out the sheet and invite students to lie down and pretend to look up at the sky to notice what kinds of shapes they see in imaginary clouds above them. Ask volunteers to tell the group what they "see" in the clouds.

Knowledge Web

As a group, discuss the book's cover, title, and author. Then, create a web with the class about what they already know about clouds, what clouds look like, and what shapes they have seen clouds form in the sky. Some children may be able to name some different varieties of clouds. (See example, right.)

After Reading

Discussion Starters

Ask students to tell you the scientific information they remember from the book. Record the list on chart paper. Then, ask children to share what they remember about the myths and record that on a separate list. Finally, ask students to come up with their own speculations about how and why clouds are formed.

Language Link

Go back through the story with the class and pick out all the words the author uses to describe clouds. There is quite a list: *high, middle, low, white, feathery, flat, puffy, small fleecy, thin milky white, gray, blue, dark, heavy,* and *tall*. Record the words on chart paper. Then, invite children to refer to the list as they describe what they know about cirrus, cumulus, and stratus clouds.

Ingredients

(FOR EACH CHILD)

1/2 cup vanilla yogurt

10 mini-marshmallows

2 tablespoons coconut, flaked

Tools & Materials

(FOR EACH CHILD)

recipe on page 45

1 small bowl (per group)

1 half-cup measuring cup (per group)

1 plastic bowl

1 plastic spoon

1 set measuring spoons (per group)

Making the Snack

Ahead of Time

Purchase large tubs of vanilla yogurt, one for each group of students to share. Place the marshmallows in small bowls, one bowl for each group.

Teaching With the Recipe

Make Connections

Consider saying something like the following: *Clouds can be fluffy, white, full of rain, full of snow, and even flat and long. Today we will make clouds that are sweet to eat and form any cloud shape you like.*

Highlight Strategies for Success

Invite volunteers to think about what will happen when they mix yogurt with the marshmallows. Ask, *Will the mixture become smooth? Why or why not?* You might say, *We're using spoons to shape our marshmallow clouds. What should we do if the marshmallows stick to the spoon?*

Revisit Learning

Before you eat, ask children to examine the marshmallow clouds they've made. Then, invite volunteers to name a few types of clouds they can spot in the sky (or in their snack bowls).

Coconut Clouds

1 Measure $\frac{1}{2}$ cup
of yogurt .

2 **Spoon** the yogurt into a bowl .

3 **Count** out 10 marshmallows .

4 **Place** the marshmallows in the bowl .

5 **Sprinkle** 2 tablespoons of coconut on top .

Planting a Rainbow

by Lois Ehlert (Harcourt, 1988)

A child and mother create a garden.
When it comes to life, their garden displays
a rainbow of colors.

Before Reading

Picnic Basket Preview

Set a copy of the book and real or silk flowers inside your basket. Introduce the story by showing the book and pointing out the brightness of the cover's colors and the words in the title of the story. Encourage children to share what they know about planting gardens. Show children the flowers from the basket and invite students to identify the different colors. Let the class know that after listening to the story they will be making a snack that will be flowers they can eat.

Knowledge Web

Introduce the story by holding up the book and having children comment on the cover and its title. Ask students, *What do you notice about this book?* Invite children to share what

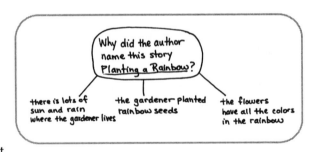

they know about plants, flowers, and rainbows. Then, ask students to predict why they think the author named this story *Planting a Rainbow*. Record their ideas on a web. (See example, above.)

After Reading

Discussion Starters

Ask children to tell you about the different ways the flowers and plants were grown in the story's garden. Ask students if any of them have ever helped plant a garden and how they did it. What did they have to do to the soil first? Did they plant bulbs, seeds, or seedlings? Record their experiences on chart paper.

Language Link

Help children go over unfamiliar words from the story, such as *soil*, *bulb*, *seedling*, and *catalog*. Many students have heard these words before but may not have a firm grasp on the meanings. Help them build some background knowledge by working as a group to develop definitions for each.

Making the Snack

Ahead of Time

Cut off the end of the celery and save the leaves. (Students will use the leaves in the last step of the recipe.) Purchase small containers of soft cream cheese or set out blocks of cream cheese to soften for an hour or so before you plan to create the snack. As this recipe is intended for children to make and eat in pairs, prepare a small bowl of cream cheese for each set of partners. Provide each table of students with celery leaves and bottles of food coloring to share.

Teaching With the Recipe

Make Connections

Consider saying something like the following: *How fun it was to learn about how all those flowers grow. What a rainbow of color! Let's make our own colorful flowers we can eat for a snack today.*

Highlight Strategies for Success

Divide the class into pairs of students. Let them know that each pair of children will be working together to prepare the snack. Invite a few volunteers to share what they know about tortillas. Then, as a group, talk about the process of rolling and cutting tortillas. Ask, *How can we spread the cream cheese and roll the tortillas so that all the cream cheese doesn't squish out the sides? How can we hold the tortillas safely while we cut them?*

Revisit Learning

Encourage students to share what they learned about flower gardens and how they bloom. You might ask, *In what ways were our flower gardens like the one in the book?*

Tortilla Pinwheel Flowers

1. Mix food coloring with 4 tablespoons of cream cheese
2. Spread the cream cheese onto a tortilla
3. Roll the tortilla
4. Use a knife to slice the roll into pieces for flowers
5. Slice celery into thin, short pieces.
6. Lay celery beneath the flowers for stems. Add leaves.

Ingredients
(FOR EACH CHILD)

1 tortilla

2 tablespoons cream cheese

1 stalk celery

Tools & Materials
(FOR EACH CHILD)

recipe on page 48

1 bowl (per group)

food coloring (per group)

2 plastic spoons

1 paper plate

Tortilla Pinwheel Flowers

1 **Mix** food coloring with 4 tablespoons of cream cheese .

2 **Spread** the cream cheese onto a tortilla .

3 **Roll** the tortilla .

4 **Use** a knife to slice the roll into pieces for flowers .

5 **Slice** celery into thin, short pieces.

6 **Lay** celery beneath the flowers for stems . Add leaves .

The Very Hungry Caterpillar

by Eric Carle (Penguin Putnam, 1969)

A very hungry caterpillar eats a week's worth of delicious food before becoming a beautiful butterfly.

Before Reading

Picnic Basket Preview

Inside your basket, tuck a copy of the book and some of the food that appeared in the story. Real fruit is easy to find (apples, pears, plums, strawberries, and oranges). If you have access to toy food, look for any of the following: a piece of chocolate cake, an ice cream cone, a pickle, a slice of Swiss cheese or salami, a lollipop, a pie, a sausage link, a cupcake, and a slice of watermelon. Introduce the book by examining the book's cover and the food with children. Discuss how some foods are healthier than others. Ask, *How would we feel if we ate all the sweet snack food in one day? Do you think we would have tummy aches? When this little caterpillar eats a lot of junk food, what do you think will happen to him?* Encourage children to make predictions about what will happen to the caterpillar in the story.

Knowledge Web

As a group, discuss the book's cover, title, and author. Have children predict with you about what will happen in the story. They may also be able to tell you potential problems the caterpillar may encounter. Ask students to share what they know about caterpillars, how they grow larger, and how they change from one thing to another. Children may be able to tell you about the four stages of a butterfly. Record their ideas on a web. (See example, right.)

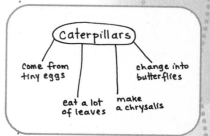

After Reading

Discussion Starters

As a group, thumb through a calendar and review the days of the week. Then, write the days of the week on chart paper. Encourage children to remember which foods the caterpillar ate on which days. Record students' answers. For more food fun, use the list to record what the children have eaten for the day. Invite volunteers to take turns listing everything they ate for either breakfast or lunch on each day of the week.

Language Link

Write the word cocoon on chart paper. Have children suggest words to describe cocoon. They may suggest cozy, warm, and soft. Explain that in the story the butterfly came from a cocoon, but that both moths and butterflies come from caterpillars and that it's moths that come from cocoons. Butterflies come from chrysalises.

Making the Snack

Ahead of Time

Begin by cutting the celery stalks in half lengthwise, into long thin strips. Then, cut the strips into thirds. Set out four bowls of ingredients for each group—peanut butter, jelly, celery, and grapes.

Teaching With the Recipe

Make Connections

Consider saying something like the following: *What a hungry caterpillar! Did that book make you hungry? It made me hungry. Let's make a healthy snack out of peanut butter and jelly. I'll show you a way to transform our sandwiches into butterflies.*

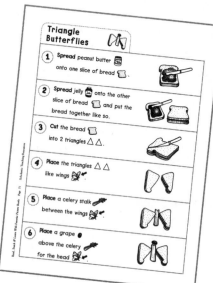

Highlight Strategies for Success

Invite volunteers to share what they know about making peanut butter and jelly sandwiches, including ways of stacking and holding the layers all together.

Revisit Learning

Encourage students to share what they learned about caterpillars and the way they change into butterflies. *We made our butterfly snacks step by step. How did the caterpillar in the story change into a butterfly? What happened first? Second?*, and so on.

Triangle Butterflies

1 **Spread** peanut butter onto one slice of bread .

2 **Spread** jelly onto the other slice of bread and put the bread together like so.

3 **Cut** the bread into 2 triangles △ △.

4 **Place** the triangles △ △ like wings .

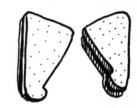

5 **Place** a celery stalk between the wings .

6 **Place** a grape above the celery for the head .

Curious George

by H. A. Rey (Houghton Mifflin, 1941)

A curious little monkey finds his way into trouble after being brought to the big city from the jungle by the man with the yellow hat.

Before Reading

Picnic Basket Preview

Put a banana and a copy of the book inside the basket. Introduce the story by pulling the book out of the basket and holding it up for the students. Ask, *What do you think this little monkey on the cover might like to eat?* After they guess, show them the banana. Explain that this story is about a monkey who is brought from the jungle to live in the city. The city will be full of adventures for him, including new ways for him to get into trouble.

Knowledge Web

As a group, discuss the book's cover, title, and author. Have students begin thinking about what a monkey might think is interesting about a city. Though some children may be familiar with the *Curious George* series, they may not remember

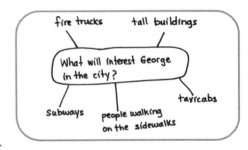

that in this first book of the series, Curious George has never before seen a city. Based on what they know about cities and about animals like monkeys, ask students to predict what types of things will interest George. Record their predictions on a web. (See example, above.)

After Reading

Discussion Starters

Invite students to name all of the ways Curious George got himself into trouble in the story. You might ask, *What happened when George tried to fly like a seagull? Tried to use the telephone? Saw the balloon man? If you were a friend of Curious George's, what advice would you give him to help him stay out of trouble in the city?*

Language Link

On chart paper, write down the word curious. Have children describe to you in their own words what it means to be curious. Record their ideas. Then ask volunteers to share some things they may be curious about.

Making the Snack

Ahead of Time

Slice each banana into six to nine slices. Either do the slicing ahead or have each child make three slices from the banana for his or her snack. Time saver: You can make the pudding and whipped cream from scratch for this recipe, but why not save time and purchase prepared pudding and whipped cream (or whipped topping)? Divide the pudding and whipped cream into bowls for each group of students to share.

Teaching With the Recipe

Make Connections

Consider saying something like the following: *George is such a curious little monkey. I'm sure he loves to eat bananas. Here's a recipe he might enjoy.*

Highlight Strategies for Success

Invite volunteers to share what they know about accurately measuring spoonfuls of gooey ingredients such as pudding and fluffy ingredients such as whipped cream. Ask, *How much is enough pudding or whipped cream? If we've scooped too much, how should we get it off our spoon?*

Revisit Learning

Encourage students to describe what Curious George was like as a character. *Would George be curious to eat one of our homemade banana cream pies? What do we know about George from our reading?* Have children give examples from the book to support their opinions.

Mini Banana Cream Pies

1. Place 1 cookie in the bottom of a baking cup.
2. Place 2 tablespoons of pudding on top of the cookie.
3. Place 3 slices of banana on top of the pudding.
4. Put 1 tablespoon of whipped cream on top.

Ingredients
(FOR EACH CHILD)

1 vanilla wafer cookie

2 tablespoons banana pudding

3 slices banana

1 tablespoon whipped cream

Tools & Materials
(FOR EACH CHILD)

recipe on page 54

2 bowls (per group)

1 baking cup

1 plastic spoon

1 paper plate

Mini Banana Cream Pies

1 **Place** 1 cookie in the bottom of a baking cup.

2 **Place** 2 tablespoons of pudding on top of the cookie.

3 **Place** 3 slices of banana on top of the pudding.

4 **Put** 1 tablespoon of whipped cream on top.

Jamberry

by Bruce Degen (HarperCollins, 1983)

A boy and a bear team up to surround themselves with all kinds of berries—blackberries, blueberries, and strawberries. Whether sailing in their "canoeberry" or dancing in meadows of strawberry jam, the two are simply content to be together in berry land.

Before Reading

Picnic Basket Preview

Inside a basket, tuck a copy of the story and a bag with a few of the different berries from the recipe (blueberries, raspberries, and strawberries). Introduce the story by holding up the colorful book cover and pointing to the happy boy and bear. Invite children to take a closer look. *Berries surround these characters. What do you think this book is about? I see a boy, a bear, and some berries. What will happen? By looking at the cover do you think this is a fiction or nonfiction book?* Show the berries and let students know that they will be using berries to make their snacks.

Knowledge Web

Point out all the different colorful berries on the book's cover and interior pages. Then, invite children to share what they know about picking and eating blueberries, raspberries, and strawberries. Record their ideas in a web. (See example, right.)

After Reading

Discussion Starters

As a group, encourage children to reflect on the story. *What were you thinking when we read about the boy and the bear dancing in meadows of strawberry jam?* Have children speculate about how they think the characters were feeling. Ask students if any of them have ever been to a meadow. *What does a meadow look and sound like?* Have them describe how they visualize meadows.

Language Link

The words *blueberries, raspberries,* and *strawberries* have something in common. Write all three words on chart paper and say each word aloud. Invite students to notice the ending these words share, "berries." As a group, look for more words in the book that have the same ending.

Ingredients

(FOR EACH CHILD)

2 tablespoons blueberries

4 tablespoons vanilla yogurt

2 tablespoons raspberries

1 tablespoon whipped cream

1 strawberry

Tools & Materials

(FOR EACH CHILD)

recipe on page 57

3 small bowls (per group)

1 set measuring spoons (per group)

1 clear plastic cup

Making the Snack

Ahead of Time

Each group of children will need a bowl of blueberries, a bowl of raspberries, a bowl of strawberries, and some yogurt. Instead of emptying large tubs of yogurt into bowls, purchase large-sized individual servings of yogurt. That way, children can measure directly out of the yogurt containers. Time saver: You can make the pudding from scratch for this recipe, but why not save time and purchase prepared pudding?

Teaching With the Recipe

Make Connections

Consider saying something like the following: *Have you ever seen as many berries as are on the pages of this book? Let's use some berries to make fancy, layered desserts for ourselves.*

Highlight Strategies for Success

Invite volunteers to share what they know about working with berries. *How can we keep them from squishing or rolling off our spoons? What should we do when a berry squishes on some clothing?*

Revisit Learning

Encourage students to share what they learned about berries. *Let's see if we can name some of the berries we cooked with or read about in the story.*

Mixed Berry Parfaits

1. Place 1 tablespoon of blueberries into a cup.
2. Place 2 tablespoons of yogurt on top of the blueberries.
3. Place 1 tablespoon of raspberries on top of the yogurt.
4. Place 2 tablespoons of yogurt on top of the raspberries.
5. Place 1 tablespoon of whipped cream on top of the yogurt.
6. Place 1 strawberry on top.

Mixed Berry Parfaits

1   **Place** 1 tablespoon

of blueberries

into a cup .

2   **Place** 2 tablespoons

of yogurt

on top of the blueberries .

3   **Place** 1 tablespoon

of raspberries

on top of the yogurt .

4   **Place** 2 tablespoons

of yogurt

on top of the raspberries .

5   **Place** 1 tablespoon

of whipped cream

on top of the yogurt .

6   **Place** 1 strawberry on top.

The Grouchy Ladybug

by Eric Carle (HarperCollins, 1977)

A grouchy ladybug begins her day by not being willing to share. After a long day of looking for someone big enough to fight, the ladybug decides that politeness has its benefits.

Before Reading

Picnic Basket Preview

Place a copy of the book inside the basket, along with the ingredients needed to make the snack—an apple, a chocolate wafer cookie, black licorice, chocolate chips, and honey. Introduce the story by asking children to describe what a ladybug looks like—color, size, etc. Then, show them the book and the ingredients in the basket. See if they can predict how you will use the ingredients to make a snack that looks like a ladybug.

Knowledge Web

As a group, discuss the book's cover, title, and author. Discuss what the word grouchy means. Ask children to share what kinds of events make them feel grouchy. Then, help students predict what might make a ladybug grouchy. Record their ideas on a web. (See example, above.)

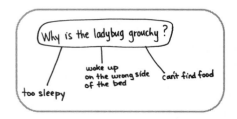

Why is the ladybug grouchy?
- too sleepy
- woke up on the wrong side of the bed
- can't find food

After Reading

Discussion Starters

Go back through the story with the students and create a list of all the animals the grouchy ladybug runs into on her journey. Point out the ways the animals she encounters become increasingly larger. Then, invite children to describe how each of the animals the ladybug meets have body features that might be dangerous to a bug.

Language Link

Invite students to think of synonyms for the word *grouchy*. Children may offer the words *grumpy*, *crabby*, and *cranky* as synonyms. List their suggestions on chart paper and invite them to add more words to the list on the days that follow.

Making the Snack

Ahead of Time

Cut the apples lengthwise in half, and cut the licorice into pieces. For each ladybug you'll need 1 three-inch piece for between the wings and 2 one-inch pieces for antennae. Then, score down the middle of the apples with a knife. These scored lines will be where students place the licorice to make ladybug wings. It helps to provide each table of children with a squeeze bottle of honey for this project, making measuring and cleanup easier.

Teaching With the Recipe

Make Connections

Consider saying something like the following: *I'm so glad that the ladybug decided to become happy and polite instead of grouchy. Let's make our own ladybugs in her honor.*

Highlight Strategies for Success

Invite volunteers to share what they know about working with sticky ingredients such as honey. *How can we keep the honey on the spoon and off our fingers? How should we spread the honey so that it covers the apple?*

Revisit Learning

Encourage students to share what they have learned about feelings. You might lead the discussion by describing what makes you grouchy. *Sometimes having sticky fingers makes me grouchy like the ladybug. I'm glad I was careful while I was making my snack. Let's think of some other ways we could keep from becoming grouchy like the ladybug.*

Ingredients
(FOR EACH CHILD)

1/2 red apple

1 chocolate wafer cookie

1 tablespoon honey

10 raisins

5 inches black shoestring licorice

Tools & Materials
(FOR EACH CHILD)

recipe on page 60

1 plastic butter knife

1 paper plate

Ladybug Apples

1. Spread honey on the apple

2. Place raisins on the apple

3. Lay licorice in the middle to make wings

4. Put the cookie halfway under the apple for the head

5. Lay licorice above the cookie for feelers

Ladybug Apples

1 **Spread** honey 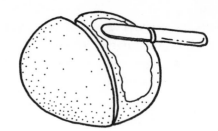 on the apple 🍎 .

2 **Place** raisins  on the apple 🍎 .

3 **Lay** licorice ╱ in the middle to make wings .

4 **Put** the cookie ⬤ halfway under the apple 🍎 for the head .

5 **Lay** licorice above the cookie ⬤ for feelers .

The Legend of the Indian Paintbrush

by Tomie dePaola (Penguin, 1988)

A young boy learns how to use his natural talent.

Before Reading

Picnic Basket Preview

Place a copy of the story, a small blanket, and a bag of tortillas inside the basket. Instead of reading the story from your usual reading chair, lay out the blanket to sit on as you introduce and later read the story. Begin by letting students know that for a long time people have been telling stories to entertain and teach each other and that storytellers sometimes read from books and sometimes share stories from memory. Explain that many Native American peoples continue to come together around campfires to share stories, and that as a group you will be pretending to be telling a story around a campfire. Then, show the cover of the book and discuss the illustration on its cover. Ask, *What do you think this book will be about? What do think an Indian paintbrush is? A legend?* Show children the bag of tortillas and invite children to offer predictions about the book. Let students know that they will be using tortillas to make a snack.

Knowledge Web

As a group, discuss the book's cover, title, and author. Invite students to share what they know about some of the artwork created by Native American peoples. Then, ask children to think about what tools and materials Native American peoples might have used to create different types of art. Record their suggestions in a web. (See example, right.)

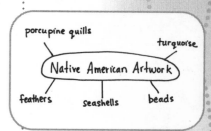

After Reading

Discussion Starters

Talk with children about how people have different talents and gifts, that some of us are good at certain things and other people are good at other things. Explain that Little Gopher felt different from the boys who could hunt and bring food back for their people. He wanted to be able to give to his people too, and he just needed to find a way to share his gift and talent with others. Ask volunteers to tell something that they enjoy doing in which they excel.

Language Link

Go back through the story and discuss words that are not familiar to students. For example, children just beginning to learn about different Native American peoples and their traditions might find buckskin and dream vision unfamiliar. As a class, create a list of unfamiliar words. Discuss how the words were used in the story and develop a definition for each.

Making the Snack

Ahead of Time

Set the butter out early in the day, so that it softens enough for easy spreading. To make distributing sugar on the tortillas easier for children, put the colored sugars inside saltshakers. If you don't have access to shakers, make them. Create small punctures in the metal top of any small condiment container or baby-food jar by using a hammer and narrow nails. (Decorative colored sugars are available in the baking aisle of most supermarkets.)

Teaching With the Recipe

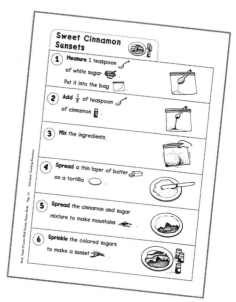

Make Connections

Consider saying something like the following: *Little Gopher brought the colors of the sunset down from the sky and to his people. We can use some of the same colors to create a sunset snack we can eat. You will be sprinkling colored sugar onto tortillas to create pictures. The tortilla will take the place of Little Gopher's buckskin. The cinnamon sugar will become the mountains. The red, yellow, and orange sugars will become the sunset.*

Highlight Strategies for Success

Invite volunteers to share what they know about sprinkling colored sugar and squeezing food-coloring bottles gently. *How much sugar is enough? How can we make sure we use just one drop from each bottle?*

Revisit Learning

Encourage students to talk about how Little Gopher made his paintings on buckskin. You might ask, *In what ways are the snacks we made like the pictures Little Gopher painted for his people?*

Ingredients

(FOR EACH CHILD)

1 tablespoon white sugar

1/8 tablespoon cinnamon

1 tablespoon butter

1 tortilla

1 tablespoon red sugar

1 tablespoon orange sugar

1 tablespoon yellow sugar

Tools & Materials

(FOR EACH CHILD)

recipe on page 63

1 set measuring spoons (per group)

1 self-sealing plastic sandwich bags

1 paper plate

Sweet Cinnamon Sunsets

1 **Measure** 1 teaspoon

of white sugar .

Put it into the bag .

2 **Add** $\frac{1}{8}$ of teaspoon

of cinnamon .

3 **Mix** the ingredients.

4 **Spread** a thin layer of butter

on a tortilla .

5 **Spread** the cinnamon and sugar

mixture to make mountains .

6 **Sprinkle** the colored sugars

to make a sunset .

Chef Hat